Original title:
Life Is a Mystery Novel with No Ending

Copyright © 2025 Creative Arts Management OÜ
All rights reserved.

Author: Lorenzo Barrett
ISBN HARDBACK: 978-1-80566-082-8
ISBN PAPERBACK: 978-1-80566-377-5

Characters Yet to Be Defined

In a world where ducks wear hats,
And cats recite Shakespeare's spats,
A detective with two left feet,
Chases shadows, oh what a feat!

Plot twists come wrapped in string,
Where every newspaper's from spring.
The baker knows more than he lets out,
While the fish just swims about.

The Last Page Unturned

I reached for the final line,
But it vanished like good wine.
An unfinished thought on a shelf,
Just like my attempts at wealth.

Characters giggle in the dark,
Wondering where they're bound to spark.
With coffee spills and dashes of flair,
What happens next? Does anyone care?

Journeys Through the Unseen

On a road made of orange peels,
With a map drawn in spaghetti meals.
I drove my car made of jelly beans,
Hoping to find what fortune means.

A squirrel in a tux took the wheel,
As the GPS spun like a wheel.
We stopped to dance with sidewalk chalk,
In a world where no secrets block.

Enigmas Beneath the Surface

Underneath the pond so green,
Lie mysteries, some hard to glean.
The frogs debate on funky tunes,
While turtles hide their little spoons.

What's that noise? A wink and a nudge,
The goldfish might just hold a grudge.
In this tale where waters swirl,
Nothing's clear; just watch it twirl.

Secrets Among the Pages

In the library, whispers grow,
Shh! Can't let the secrets flow.
Plot twists lurking round each bend,
Who knew the cat would be my friend?

Characters lost in silly fights,
Chasing clues through sleepless nights.
A detective dressed in polka dots,
Solving crimes while giggling lots.

Infinite words spill everywhere,
Witty puns hang in the air.
A twist of fate, a laugh so grand,
Plot holes filled with goofy sand.

Ink spills with a humorous wink,
As the plot dares me to think.
Each chapter leads to a new jest,
Unanswered questions, but I jest!

The Endless Quest for Meaning

In pursuit of wisdom, we roam,
Chasing shadows, far from home.
With a magnifying glass in hand,
Searching for clues, made of sand.

Philosophers, they ponder deep,
While revelers dance, and secrets creep.
A riddle wrapped in jellybeans,
What could it mean? Oh, who knows what it means!

Life's absurd in this funny chase,
With rubber chickens all in place.
Searching high, then down we look,
Did I lose my plot in this book?

Every answer leads to more,
What was that noise behind the door?
I laugh it off, let's not be serious,
This quest for sense is becoming curious!

The Last Chapter Unwritten

The ink runs dry, yet stories thrive,
Characters dance, somehow alive.
But wait! Is that a plot twist rare?
I thought I lost them, but they're right there!

The final line, yet no one knows,
Will they kiss, or maybe throw blows?
The script remains a barren page,
Filled with humor, age to age.

Readers chuckle at every turn,
Waiting for lessons, oh, how they yearn!
But what's the rush, let's just have fun,
A story's journey has just begun.

So let us scribble with glee and might,
Life's a joke, a funny sight.
The end is just a funny tease,
Or maybe it's just a sneeze!

Crossroads of the Heart's Page

At the crossroads stood a cat,
Wearing a hat and looking fat.
He pondered paths as birds flew by,
Sipping tea and letting out a sigh.

A squirrel jested, quite a flair,
Challenging fate with a daring stare.
"Choose the left or the right route,
But do watch out for the loony lout!"

They laughed at chance, both bold and spry,
With riddles that could make you cry.
Yet in their hearts, the truth hung tight,
That endings may start with a curious bite.

So off they trotted, a quirky crew,
In search of laughter, in skies so blue.
For who needs answers to know the fun?
Each twist and turn, just more to shun!

The Unfinished Symphony of Now

A jazz tune played on a lazy afternoon,
With ducks that danced to a whimsical tune.
The notes flew high, yet fell so low,
In the middle, a pie made for show.

The conductor's lost in a nod and a wink,
While sheep in tuxedos sketch and think.
Each note a chance, a silly dare,
Life's plot thickens in the open air.

The audience giggles at an inside jest,
As dogs play cards, and the cats invest.
The symphony swirled, never complete,
With each little step, the laughter's sweet.

So play on, friends, in the swirling breeze,
With every moment, just aim to please.
For in this dance, absurdity shines,
And every misstep becomes the fine lines!

A Script Without Resolution

Every page is a riddle, a twist in the tale,
Characters jump, some laugh, some pale.
The villain is sneaky, the hero's a clown,
In the end, we all slip, then tumble right down.

Plot holes like donuts, all sugary bright,
We chase after shadows, try to get it right.
But every conclusion is just more surprise,
With endings so funny, we can't roll our eyes.

The Puzzles We Carry

We all hold a puzzle, missing a piece,
A cat wearing glasses, a horse dressed with fleece.
We scramble and fumble, search high and low,
Each clue just a joke at the end of the show.

Every question's a giggle, a chuckle or two,
Chasing our tails like we've got nothing new.
The answers are silly, wrapped in a jest,
Life's a grand puzzle that never gets pressed.

Echoes of What Remains

Echoes of laughter dangle on strings,
Muffled by secrets that nonsense brings.
Whispering stories of what could have been,
With characters dancing, a charming routine.

In shadows of chapters, we trip on a rhyme,
Every moment ridiculous, fall with a chime.
The plot thickens sweetly, like jam on a toast,
In this timeless escapade, we're all just a ghost.

A Tale that Bends and Twists

A tale that bends like a pretzel so bold,
With punchlines so tasty, they never get old.
Each chapter a rollercoaster, up and down sway,
Characters tumble, goofing all the way.

We snicker at mysteries that escape all our grasp,
Each twist leaves us giggling, it's all just a rasp.
So pour another coffee, we're here for the fun,
In this crazy adventure, we've only just begun.

Traces of Footsteps Unseen

In wedged shoes I wander, carefree,
Each step a hilarious calamity.
The floor's a stage for my misstep dance,
With every twist, I take a chance.

Invisible paths where laughter lies,
Who's left their mark beneath the skies?
A pizza slice dripped on the floor,
Guess it's just pizza, nothing more.

Enigmas of the Everyday

Why's my sock always missing one?
Is it abducted? Oh, what fun!
The toast burns on a sunny day,
Spontaneous char, just my buffet.

I found a hairpin in my shoe,
How did it get there? No clue!
Hats that disappear in thin air,
A conundrum I've learned to bear.

Fables Without Resolutions

The cat plots grand escape at night,
No one believes her, what a fright!
She stares outside, wide-eyed and bold,
Dreaming of treasures and tales untold.

I wrote a letter to my fridge,
It replied with a frosty smidge.
No ending found, just hungry ghosts,
Who knew the fridge could offer toasts?

The Manuscript of Memories

A spilled drink tells a story grand,
Of parties lost and dance unplanned.
I scribble notes in sticky pads,
Decorated by my silly fads.

Forgotten toys from days of yore,
Voices echo from the floor.
Old photos reveal forgotten styles,
Each laugh a chapter, caught for miles.

Threading Through the Unknown

In shadows where secrets play,
A cat's meow leads us astray,
With each turn, a giggle hides,
Who knew truth wears such odd strides?

We stroll through plots of twisty fate,
Oh, what a riddle, isn't it great?
The coffee spills, the pages turn,
In every laugh, a lesson learned.

The clues are lost and so am I,
Wait, was that a llama? Oh my!
Fate's humor hugs, a cheeky friend,
We'll chase the quirk until the end.

With mismatched socks and silly hats,
We chase the tales like playful cats,
Every day's a scribbled page,
A story penned with wit and rage.

Sentences Yet to be Spoken

There's a joke in the air, can you hear?
It's woven with laughter, tinged with cheer,
Words dance like butterflies on a spree,
Leaving thoughts blurred as they flee.

Scribbled notes flutter down like leaves,
Each one a riddle that never deceives,
But don't hold your breath, just let it go,
What's unsaid is the star of the show.

We trip over puns like they're the floor,
Yet stumble on wisdom, oh what a lore,
Each giggle a thread, slightly unspooled,\nIn this tale, we are perfectly fooled.

With ticklish whispers and nudges of fate,
The punchline's a cliff, don't hesitate,
The story keeps twisting in wild spree,
Yet the best punchlines are still yet to be.

The Cryptic Dance of Days

Time's a waltz on a wobbly stage,
With each step written on a worn page,
A jester prances with a silly grin,
Making sense of the chaos within.

Mornings start with a puzzled glance,
Is that coffee, or a chance to prance?
Dinners are riddles wrapped in delight,
Who knew soup could take flight at night?

Every sunrise, a riddle indeed,
With ducks in bow ties, oh what a lead,
Spin in circles, embrace the odd,
And remember, it's well worth the nod.

So twirl with me in this awkward ballet,
We'll laugh through the glitches, come what may,
In this cryptic dance, let's find our way,
For every mystery is just a play.

Lives Entwined in Enigma

We weave our tales like spaghetti strands,
In a pot of mysteries, oh how it stands,
Each twist a giggle, each fork a tease,
Who knew the sauce could bring such ease?

Neighbors wear costumes of their own lore,
A pirate next door, with treasure galore,
Their stories collide in a bizarre embrace,
A jigsaw of chaos, a wild rat race.

Every secret shared is a piece of the pie,
While socks go missing, oh me, oh my,
The absurdity blooms, like flowers in spring,
Life's odd little treasures, what joy they bring!

So join in the fun, let's make it a spree,
As we untangle this curious mystery,
For wrapped in the odd, we find a spree,
In every enigma, there's laughter, you see.

Choices on a Whimsical Page

In the book of quirky twists,
You choose a door, it's hard to miss.
A purple rabbit, a dancing cat,
Each turn is ruled, by this and that.

With pancakes flying, who needs a plot?
A wise old turtle gives advice—so not!
Flip a coin or take a dive,
In this tale, it's fun to thrive.

The heroine's shoes are two left feet,
But watch her shine, she can't be beat.
In socks of polka, she finds her way,
Tomorrow's humor's like yesterday's play.

So grab your pen, let's write tonight,
We'll scribble in laughter, with pure delight.
Each silly choice turns dread to glee,
In our story, be wild and free!

Signatures of an Untold Fate

In the margins of fate, you find your name,
If only the stars would play the same game.
A funny signature, squiggles and dots,
Meet the lost socks, and the coffee pots.

With a wink from fate, you take the plunge,
"Follow that chicken!" says the grumpy lunge.
It pecks the rules, but they all agree,
It's better with laughter, just wait and see.

Cupcakes tumble as plans go rogue,
Each recipe calls for a bullfrog's fog.
The toaster's giggles fill the air,
Who knew a kitchen could be so rare?

Doodles of destiny start to dance,
In the chaos, we all take a chance.
The pen runs dry, and that's just fine,
For the fun is in knowing, we're all divine!

The Infinite Index of Possibilities

Pages flutter with whimsical schemes,
Each day unveils new plot-driven dreams.
A pirate with poodles in a hot air fight,
Searching for treasure at the speed of light.

The index laughs, so much to explore,
Upon each chapter, laugh a little more.
From ice cream castles to plots gone wrong,
Each possibility sings a silly song.

Time machines made from cardboard and tape,
You'll find a hero in the shape of a grape.
With a rallying cry, and a confetti blast,
History spins in circles, oh what a contrast!

So mark your path with quirky delight,
Choose every adventure that's ever in sight.
For a tale without end is quite the thrill,
Embrace the chaos and dance at will!

The Laughter of Hidden Chapters

Turn the page, there's laughter to find,
A treasure of giggles, oh so unlined.
Hidden chapters with quirky delights,
Where marshmallows fight in epic bites.

The villain's sipping tea, quite absurd,
Plot twists fly like a silly bird.
A pirate and fairy share a sweet laugh,
In this story, it's a ridiculous path.

Mysteries giggle, then vanish away,
Both shadows and sunshine are here to stay.
For every wrong turn leads to a smile,
Time to kick back and ponder for a while.

So gather your friends for a read-aloud,
Let the joys of this tale draw a crowd.
With laughter and whimsy, we'll find our way,
In chapters unknown, let's brighten the day!

Tales of the Invisible Threads

In shadows cast by fables told,
A cat sleeps curled, as stories unfold.
The socks are lost, a game of chance,
As mismatched pairs lead a funny dance.

A cup of tea, a tale awry,
The teabag whispers, 'Why so shy?'
A kettle sings, though no one hears,
As laughter bubbles, dispelling fears.

A fork and knife debate their fate,
On leftover food, they can't wait.
Each meal a clue, each bite a twist,
In banquet halls where memories persist.

Where breadcrumbs mark the secret paths,
And laughter echoes in aftermaths.
With tangled threads of silly quests,
Each turn reveals what fun suggests.

Eclipses of Understanding

With moons that giggle and suns that pout,
Knowledge plays hide and seek, no doubt.
Questions swirl like butterflies,
In a garden where reason often flies.

A book once closed, now slightly ajar,
Whispers of wisdom from a distant star.
The plot thickens like grandma's stew,
With kooky characters and antics too.

Silly rumors bounce like a ball,
In the corridors of the great hall.
A wink, a nod, a wink in return,
For answers, it seems, we shall always yearn.

So chase the clues on merry legs,
Through tangled thoughts and playful pegs.
In the cosmic joke where we all partake,
Understanding laps like waves on a lake.

Signposts in the Fog

Clouds of confusion, a misty spree,
Where signposts sway like a drunken tree.
One way to here and the other to there,
A compass laughs, 'Oh, don't you dare!'

The map is scribbled with doodles bright,
Directions written in the dead of night.
With arrows bending, curving around,
Leading us back to where we are bound.

A riddle wrapped in a family joke,
Tucked in the hugs that never choke.
A laugh, a grin, as we lose our way,
Turning confusion into a ballet.

So dance in the fog, twirl with delight,
For every wrong turn leads to bright light.
With signposts of laughter guiding us true,
We stumble and giggle in the morning dew.

Chronicles in the Marginalia

In margins wide where thoughts collide,
Scribbles of nonsense take a joyful ride.
With doodles and jests, the pages gleam,
Each comment whispers a secret dream.

A cheeky note from a friend afar,
'You left your keys in the buzzy car!'
With arrows pointing to where they lay,
Chronicles penned in a funny way.

And footnotes shimmer with audacious flair,
A dragon danced on a chair with care.
Each line a giggle, each word a jest,
In the stories we write, we find our best.

So flip through the pages, take time to roam,
In the margins dwell, make it your home.
For in the scribbles of laughter and play,
There's a mystery woven in every day.

The Incomplete Narrative

Once upon a time, or so they claim,
A cat in a hat played a silly game.
The hero forgot how to tie his shoes,
While villains debated on what to choose.

A plot twist occurred, but nobody cared,
The prologue was funny, the ending was spared.
Characters laughed, though they weren't quite right,
And the audience chuckled at their silly fight.

Pages were missing, the ink ran dry,
The villain slipped on a banana pie.
Who killed the butler? Oh, what a bore,
He's living in Bali, never seen anymore.

So raise a glass to the tale we ignore,
With gumdrops and giggles that leave us wanting more.
The ending's a riddle that no one can find,
And that's how we write with a comical mind.

Mysterious Footprints in the Sand

Footprints appear where none should have been,
A crab took a stroll, just as I'd seen.
Sandy detectives with nothing to trace,
Are trying to figure out this lost race.

The tide rolls in, and the tale gets wet,
With seashell suspects and a floppy pet.
So many questions with humor entwined,
Like, where did the duck with a cape come to find?

Laughter erupts as we try to perceive,
The story that hides when the sun starts to leave.
Were they here for a picnic, a treasure to find?
Or just a lost party for a whale unconfined?

Each swipe of the wave erases the clue,
The mystery deepens, and we're left in a stew.
But let's not forget, as we clean up the sand,
It's all just a giggle, a mere grain unplanned.

Chapters Lost in the Fog

In a foggy town where stories grow shy,
An author forgot how to wave goodbye.
Lost in the mist, characters roam,
Wondering if this was ever their home.

A parrot squawks tales with a twist at the end,
While the plot ducks through to meet a new friend.
Chapters distorted like candy on a stick,
Plot devices waddling, a humorous trick.

Their dialogue drips with misplaced intent,
Like a sandwich composed of an unshaped mint.
As the fog lifts, nothing comes clear,
Characters laugh at their own wild fear.

So pour out some coffee, let's sip on our fate,
With stories awry that we chuckle to rate.
Each chapter a giggle, as we turn the page,
In this joyous confusion, we smile and engage.

The Unfinished Symphony of Days

There once was a fiddle that played on its own,
But the bow went AWOL, and the strings were overgrown.
Each note was a hiccup, each pause a surprise,
As the townsfolk danced under two sunny skies.

The composer just shrugged, all chuckles and cheer,
Lost in the rhythm, he forgot how to steer.
Ba-dum, ba-dum, what a curious tune,
Intermission forever, like a laugh with no swoon.

Each day was a note, some sharp and some flat,
As musicians spilled coffee, fell into a chat.
The score was incomplete, yet joy overflowed,
For every odd blunder, new laughter bestowed.

So when the sun sets, and the night fills the air,
We'll sing an off-key song without any care.
With symphonies silly, let's dance through the haze,
As each moment is bright, in this unfinished craze.

Unwritten Destinies in the Stars

In the sky, a tale unfolds,
Characters lost, yet bold.
With every twist, a giggle rises,
Plot holes hide ridiculous surprises.

Galactic gaffes on a cosmic stage,
Aliens dance, write the next page.
Chasing dreams with wayward maps,
Our futures await, perhaps with mishaps.

Stars conspire with playful gleams,
Whispering secrets, chuckling schemes.
Fate scribbles notes in a buzzing bar,
Interrupting destinies we can't quite spar.

So toast to the chaos and whimsy too,
For tomorrow's chapter may flip the view.
In this glorious mess, we all shall play,
As the constellations lead us astray!

The Mystery of the Wandering Heart

With a skip and a hop, I pursue my love,
A heart that dances, a gift from above.
Does it wander alone, or lead me in jest?
A comic chase, my heart's on a quest.

Each beat is a riddle, each flutter a clue,
It zigzags so wildly, I can't keep in view.
Romance in chaos, the script's all askew,
But giggles confirm, it's absurd but it's true.

Maps leading nowhere, signs point to cheese,
Love's pretty puzzling like a bad-toothed tease.
Yet in all the knots, laughter is found,
As my tender heart wobbles around.

So here's to the runners, the lovers, the clowns,
Who chase after joy, wearing mismatched crowns.
In this playful caper, I find my own art,
As I dance with the mystery of my own wandering heart!

Tangled Narratives of Existence

Threads of stories twist and twine,
In this yarn of life, nothing's quite fine.
Plot lines tangle, oh what a spree,
Characters lost in a cup of green tea.

Each morning I wake to a fresh plot hole,
Grasping for sense, but losing control.
Eavesdropping on drama from the next door,
As my dreams push me out, always wanting more.

Humor lives here in the pages we turn,
With every slip, we all get to learn.
Dance with the chaos, chuckle a beat,
Find joy in the mess, it's all quite a treat.

So join me, dear reader, on this wild ride,
A journey so funny, we won't need to hide.
In tangled narratives, we'll laugh and we'll play,
As life scribbles stories in its own quirky way!

The Open Canvas of Tomorrow

A blank slate awaits with colors so bright,
Doodles of nonsense, pure morning delight.
Splatters of dreams, with giggles and sighs,
Creating a tapestry where oddness complies.

Each stroke is a jest, every hue is a laugh,
Sketching my journey, a nonsensical path.
Brushes of fate flick paint like a dart,
As I navigate chaos with an open heart.

Tomorrow's just waiting for pranks to unfold,
An artist's delight in stories retold.
So scribble away, unconfined and free,
On this canvas of life, be as silly as can be.

With each quirky curve, let worries dissolve,
In the gallery of time, we'll merrily evolve.
From wild imaginings, we'll celebrate cheer,
In the open canvas, let's all persevere!

The Labyrinth of Choices

In a maze of options wide,
I took a left when I should've tried.
The signs are funny, all askew,
A map that changes with each clue.

Do I stop for ice cream or go ahead?
Decisions spin inside my head.
Each fork in the road, a twisty plot,
With silly turns I've often fought.

A squirrel just laughed, quite bold and spry,
Mocking my quest as I passed by.
Was that a sign or mere delight?
I giggled under the soft moonlight.

At the end, I found a cake,
For every choice I've had to make.
With frosting layers, sweet and bright,
Cheers to the whims of day and night!

Beyond the Final Whispers

The curtain falls but who knows why,
A plot twist just made me sigh.
Characters pop back in and out,
The ending's lost, of this no doubt.

A glass slipper? I'll pass, I cheer,
What if I trip and face my fear?
I tumble down a rabbit hole,
With riddles that tickle my very soul.

Beyond the whispers, secrets tease,
Are these the answers? Oh, please seize!
I chase the shadows, they prance and dance,
What nonsense we weave in this curious chance!

The last page turns, a laugh, a groan,
Characters leave but I'll hold my own.
For in this book, I'm the star,
With open endings near and far!

Echoes of Forgotten Stories

In dusty corners, tales reside,
Forgotten treasures, time's great tide.
With pages yellowed, still they grin,
Spinning yarns of chaos, out and in.

A pirate's parrot, a nervous laugh,
"Here be treasure!" but it's just a gaffe.
The knight forgot his trusty steed,
Now he's a hero lost in his weed.

The echoes call, "Remember me?"
As I giggle at their wild spree.
Characters rush back, full of cheer,
Complicated plots? Let's grab a beer!

Each story blends, a wild embrace,
Turns silly drama into a race.
In the end, we'll toast this mess,
And rewrite the script with no stress!

The Unseen Connections

In crowded rooms, a wink exchanged,
A twist of fate, nothing arranged.
With mischief afoot, a dance unfolds,
Where laughter's the mystery everyone holds.

A cousin's friend makes coffee strong,
But spills the beans in the form of song.
With every sip, more secrets bared,
Connections deepened and none prepared.

The plot thickens with pies and cake,
Is this dessert or a high-stakes stake?
Each crumb a clue in this grand charade,
Who knew joy could come with such a parade?

As the evening fades, we raise a glass,
"To unseen ties, let's make them last!"
For in every laugh, a bond is spun,
A whimsical puzzle, all in fun!

Unwritten Pages of Existence

In the attic of chance, a book gathers dust,
Each page blank, yet filled with trust.
The pen dances wildly, despair to elation,
Typing out nonsense, a grand exploration.

Tea spills in outrage, as plot twists unfold,
Characters mishap, their antics so bold.
A cat in a hat, atop a grand throne,
Meows at the reader, 'You're not alone!'

The Chapter That Never Closes

Turn and return, it's a loop-de-loop,
Missed the last page? Join the troupe!
Authors are napping, they snooze through the tale,
While we chase after breadcrumbs, beyond the pale.

The villain just tripped, in a big plot twist,
But no one's around, who gets the last gist?
Let's frolic in chaos, streamers in hand,
The sequel's on hold, isn't life just grand?

Whispers of the Unfolding Tale

In the margins, notes whisper, 'Don't you fret!'
Each line a riddle, a joke, a pet.
A hero with hiccups, a sidekick with flair,
They tumble through pages with raucous despair.

Plot holes like swimming pools, deep and wide,
Diving right in for a hilarity ride.
As quips fizz like soda, laughter takes flight,
In the absurdity, everything feels right.

Shadows of Yesterday

Once upon a time, in a land made of cheese,
Characters puzzled, not knowing to please.
The side-stories linger, like echoes of joy,
A rubber chicken juggles, a mischievous toy.

Glimpses of futures with topsy-turvy twists,
Plotting their schemes, in wink and in mists.
Yesterday's shadows dance jigs on the floor,
As the bookkeeper chuckles, our tales to explore.

Secrets of Tomorrow

Turn the key, what's behind that door?
A world waiting here, a magical lore.
Balloons filled with laughter, and fables to share,
Tomorrow's surprises, just hanging in air.

A sock with the secrets, a shoe with a song,
Guiding us forward, where we all belong.
So keep flipping pages, let mischief be free,
In this book of wonder, just wait and see!

Whispers in the Margins

In the margins, notes do dance,
A scribble here, a cheeky glance.
Plot twists sneak behind the page,
Characters act like they're on stage.

The cat's the villain, or so it seems,
Chasing shadows of our dreams.
Chapters shifted with a laugh,
Life's a puzzle, a witty gaffe.

Coffee stains and lines askew,
Hints dropped like breadcrumbs too.
Every failure's a jolly jest,
Crafting stories we love best.

Twists and turns with laughter loud,
Each misstep, we're feeling proud.
In this book where laughter lingers,
Wit and wisdom dance on fingers.

Shadows of Unfolding Pages

In shadows where the secrets creep,
The bookworms say, 'Don't lose sleep!'
Flipping pages, tales collide,
With every twist, we'll take a ride.

The plot thickens like grandma's stew,
Characters vibrant, dressed in blue.
With every turn, a giggle springs,
Oh, the joy of unexpected flings!

Lost in chapters, never found,
The drama's silly, but we're spellbound.
Witty banter fills the air,
Life's a book, don't you dare share!

A mystery wrapped in a riddle's friend,
Where every laugh could start a trend.
These pages hold a dance of glee,
As shadows swirl in sweet decree.

The Plot Twists of Existence

The plot twists like a rubber band,
Where heroes trip, and sidekicks stand.
Chapters filled with silly tales,
Adventures where laughter never pales.

Characters mumble long-lost truths,
While sneaky squirrels steal our boots.
The villain struts with shoes untied,
We're the jesters, enjoying the ride.

An author giggles, ink on their hands,
Crafting chaos with clever plans.
With every turn of the page we cheer,
For the unexpected joys appear!

So laugh along with every scheme,
As life's absurd and filled with dreams.
In this quirky tale, we dare to fly,
From cliffhangers that make us sigh!

Epilogue in the Unknown

In the end, what do we find?
An epilogue that's quite unrefined.
With fuzzy plots and plot holes wide,
We shrug and grin, still take the ride.

The characters bow, but do they leave?
Or stick around? Who'd believe?
In this tale, nothing really ends,
New stories come, as laughter sends.

So we scribble notes and turn the page,
Searching for wisdom in our age.
Plot lines tangled like spaghetti strands,
Yet joy remains in all our plans.

Together we weave this merry dance,
In chapters where we laugh and prance.
An epilogue made with a wink and grin,
In this book, we always win!

Pages Turned Underneath Stars

Beneath the stars, the pages flip,
The plot twists laugh as I take a sip.
Characters stumble, just like my shoe,
Could it be magic, or just a goo?

With every chapter, the coffee spills,
As I chase laughter and dodge the drills.
Ghosts and giggles dance in the night,
Each turn of phrase feels just right!

Mysteries linger, like socks left behind,
Witty remarks with each twist I find.
Adventures of owls perched on the roof,
Sharing secrets with no need for proof.

So here I sit, with pen in hand,
Writing the tales only I understand.
For in this book, under endless skies,
Every laugh carries a sweet surprise!

Secrets Beneath the Ink

In the margins, whispers softly flow,
Secrets hidden, but do they really know?
A cat with a hat, or was it a dog?
Life spills ink, like a mischievous fog.

Every scribble holds a tale untold,
While the narrator's voice seems a bit bold.
Oh what a night with biscuits on hand,
As mystery puzzles unravel the sand.

The plot thickens, like grandma's stew,
With flavors of fate, and a twist or two.
I chuckle aloud at the twists of fate,
Between the lines, I dance and create.

So grab your quill, let the stories fly,
Beneath the ink, oh my, oh my!
Each revelation is a jolly ride,
With laughs and surprises tucked inside!

The Enigma of Each Sunrise

With each sunrise, the riddles awake,
As roosters compete for their morning cake.
Carrots may talk, and squirrels wear capes,
This day might be wild in fanciful shapes.

Coffee brews wonder, as toast starts to sing,
Plot points develop, with a hint of zing.
With sunshine's warmth, laughter prevails,
Chasing shadows and sailing on sails.

As mysteries bubble in morning light,
I chase the absurd, oh what a sight!
The sun grins wide, casting playful hues,
While chairs giggle, sharing secret views.

So embrace the day, let the questions come,
For the riddle of life is just plain fun!
Beneath the hues of dawn's bright cheer,
Every moment whispers, "Stay right here!"

The Author's Invisible Hand

In shadows lurk the author's grin,
Nudging characters with a playful spin.
A wink here, a twist there, oh what a race,
Chasing plots like bunnies in an embrace.

With invisible ink and a feathered quill,
The thumbs-up moments give me a thrill.
Every chapter flows with chaotic cheer,
As the author giggles, it's music to hear.

From blunders to triumphs, all tightly bound,
Characters juggling in circus-like rounds.
Confessions from chairs and a squirrel's delight,
What absurd secrets unfold overnight?

So let the pages dance and take flight,
With the author's hand crafting pure delight.
Where laughter reigns, and the quirks all blend,
In this endless saga, there's no clear end!

Dreams Written in Shadows

In a world where whispers play,
Cacti wear hats on a sunny day.
Cats solve riddles with a sly grin,
While turtles race to see who'll win.

Lost socks dance, a curious sight,
Balloons chat on a starry night.
The clock ticks backwards, oh what a joy,
As squirrels hold court with their favorite toy.

Pancakes flip like acrobats bold,
With syrup secrets yet to be told.
Paperclips plotting a heist so grand,
In a whimsical, zany wonderland.

Behind closed doors, the shadows laugh,
Playing charades on their playful path.
As dreams unfold in colors so bright,
Life's a story, wrapped up in delight.

The Fragments of a Changed Plot

Once a hero forgot his quest,
He slipped on jelly, at best, a jest.
With sidekicks laughing, in jumbled dreams,
All had a taste of cream-filled themes.

A dragon snored while knitting a scarf,
While knights told tales that sparked a laugh.
The princess chortled at her own distress,
Trapped in a tower of knitting mess.

Maps gone missing, lost in the trees,
Pirates sing songs to a rustling breeze.
A treasure map drawn on a napkin old,
Still found its way to the plot that's bold.

Plot twists happens like bubbles that pop,
Characters skip and dance on top.
In snippets of chaos, laughter prevails,
As strange tales weave through whimsical trails.

Conundrums Beneath the Surface

Beneath the ink, where stories hide,
Puzzles dance, in a scrap of pride.
A rubber duck floats in a sea of ink,
While the plot twists faster than you think.

Leprechauns plot with their sly little tricks,
Juggling time like a bag of Magic Mix.
As banana peels spark up the floor,
The riddle of life leaves us wanting more.

Confetti rains on an unmade bed,
Ghosts play cards, with a wink and a thread.
Elevators dance between floors of fate,
Ticklish moments we all can't wait.

In the margins, the laughter spills,
As mystery bubbles with colorful thrills.
Unraveled chapters, oh what a chase,
Life's little puzzles, with a warming embrace.

The Veil of Uncertainty

A curtain flutters with whispers anew,
While robots recite poetry they brew.
Invisible quirks dance on the breeze,
Chasing after strange thoughts with ease.

The fish in the pond wear top hats and ties,
While llamas undermine with their clever lies.
On Tuesday, the cows take a stroll in style,
As gophers discuss the latest while.

Cheese wheels roll down streets of delight,
Bicycles wobble in a comical flight.
Mystery muffins bake in the night,
Filling the air with a sweet, funny fright.

Between giggles, secrets confide,
Wonders and oddities jive side by side.
The veil remains, though laughter is clear,
In a world where surprises draw near.

Pages Yet to Be Penned

Turn the page, a laugh or two,
Plot twists that leave us askew.
Characters stumble, trip and fall,
Guessing the ending, we ponder it all.

Do I wear this hat or that one bright?
A butler winks in the moonlit night.
Maybe the dog was the clever one,
Wait—was that a plot twist or just plain fun?

A coffee spill, a whistle of fate,
As we piece together this puzzling state.
Journal pages filled with ink and cheer,
Writing our tales, but never quite clear.

The Scribe of Chance Encounters

Once at the cafe, a grand mistake,
The barista laughed as my muffin did break.
Should I seek wisdom in crumbs and cream?
Or just sip coffee and continue to dream?

In the park, a frog eased my mind,
He croaked in riddles, one of a kind.
A picnic gone wild, sandwiches fly,
Time to unveil what's near and nigh.

A taxi driver with stories to tell,
Each turn of the wheel cast a quirky spell.
Is that a clue, or a simple joke?
In this tale, even pigeons provoke!

Drifting Through a World Unscripted

Oh, the chaos that colors my day,
Where socks might vanish, gone astray.
I trip on the carpet, oh what a sight—
Maybe the plot needs some light!

Dramatic pauses fill each moment,
Like narrators lost in their own foment.
Giraffes in top hats dance to a beat,
If this is a dream, it's all bittersweet.

Nonsensical whispers float through my mind,
As I search for answers, they're hard to find.
Perhaps I'm the star, or just a mere plot,
In this scripted chaos, I'm lost in the lot!

Journeys Embroidered with Doubt

Step right up, the show is grand,
A map of mishaps, all unplanned.
What's the next chapter, I cannot say,
Just follow the breadcrumbs and hope for day.

Like a turtle who thinks he can't run,
Each obstacle's just a chance for fun.
I'll wear a cape, let's fly through the grind,
Spinning circles, I've lost my mind!

With every choice, a giggle appears,
As I dance with doubt, through laughter and tears.
A cat in my hat, so wise, so sly,
In each crazy venture, I'm ready to fly!

Encounters Written in the Stars

Under a sky so bright and wide,
Fate plays tag, we're on for the ride.
Aliens peek from a comet's tail,
Laughing at us, like we're the joke in their tale.

Meteor showers sprinkle our paths,
As we dance through cosmic math.
Each glance a twist, a plot unfold,
Who knew stardust had tales to be told?

We bump into quirks and oddities,
Local rulers with curious philosophies.
With each encounter, a chuckle erupts,
In this dazzling universe, hilarity disrupts.

Stars wink knowingly, they know the plot,
We're but pawns in a celestial knot.
So let's raise toast to these galactic scenes,
For every misstep, the universe beams.

Envelopes of Curiosity

In a world where words take flight,
I find envelopes of mysteries at night.
Each note a laugh, a riddle to solve,
Like Monopoly players, we evolve!

Open one, and it's a silly truth,
Like socks and sandals: a fashion sleuth.
Check the next, it's a cat's grand plan,
To rule the world from a cozy can.

With stamps that giggle and winks that play,
The postman's jokes brighten my day.
Unraveling quirks in each paper fold,
A hidden treasure, if only bold!

Curiosity drives my clumsy quest,
Every envelope a brand-new jest.
And as I shuffle through each silly clue,
Life's a comedy, in every hue!

Forks in the Road of Fate

A fork in the road, what shall I eat?
Pasta or pizza? Decisions so sweet!
Each path a twist, with toppings galore,
Yet somehow I end up munching on more.

Left leads to laughter, right heads to woe,
Each step a skip, oh where should I go?
With every turn, a new plot does thicken,
Like playing charades, where everyone's stricken.

Coffee shop brawls over who makes the best,
An ongoing debate, and we're all so blessed.
Then off to a dance with a quirky old cat,
Who teaches us moves that look like a spat.

So here I stand, at the next funny fork,
Should I join the circus or just nibble on pork?
Every choice is a giggle, a twist of fate,
The fun is the journey, so let's eat on plate!

The Library of Untold Dreams

Upon the shelves, secrets lay tight,
Books with covers that spark a delight.
Each tale a tickle, a mystery sly,
Where every chapter's a wink to the sky.

Curling up cozy, I grab a good read,
Each page unfolds a whimsical deed.
Knights and dragons, in battle they swing,
But often I find they're just playing king.

The librarian winks with a mischievous flair,
Hiding fun plots in the dusty cool air.
For every "Once upon a time" stands in line,
A punchline waiting, oh isn't that fine?

So I'll wander these isles, giggly and bright,
For dreams penned in prose spark joy and delight.
In this library, laughter's the theme,
As every bedtime story whispers a dream!

A Journey Through Mysterious Words

In a world where plot twists loom,
Characters wear hats, and brushes bloom.
Each page a riddle, a cheeky clue,
Falling flat, but we laugh, it's true.

The hero trips over shoelace tales,
Chasing shadows with grand, wild wails.
A chapter ending with a pie in the face,
Oh, what a laugh in this plot-filled race!

Sidekicks in socks that mismatch in style,
Skating on laughs, oh what a while!
With every turn, a chuckle or two,
Each mystery wrapped in silly déjà vu.

So grab your pen and join the spree,
In this whimsical journey, we're all free.
Ink spills stories, both quirky and bright,
In tales that tickle, bring pure delight.

Inkblots of Untold Journeys

A coffee stain shapes a secret path,
As we giggle through absurd aftermath.
The author chuckles from their cozy chair,
An inkblot pirate sails—we're unaware!

A button lost, found in a grand old tome,
Who needs a map, when you've got a poem?
With riddles tossed and lines all askew,
Each step a giggle, all else is askew.

An umbrella blooms in the middle of June,
While cats in capes plot a heist in the moon.
Oh, what a ride in this whimsical land,
Every chapter's wish is just slightly unplanned!

So ink your adventures, don't fret or pout,
Every good mystery is just a thought cloud.
The journey unfolds with a wink and a jest,
In untold tales where nonsense feels best.

Unwritten Lines of Destiny

The script is blank on a page so white,
But a rubber chicken gives us a fright.
Jokes spill out from corners unseen,
As plot lines dance in a wobbly scene.

Cups overflow with coffee and dreams,
Characters leap through laughter and screams.
Each 'to be continued' brings a grin,
With every new twist, we all dive in.

So let's write tales of things gone awry,
While chortling at how the pigeons fly high.
In this unwritten space of clumsy rhyme,
Destiny chuckles, taking its time.

So grab that quill and start your own show,
What joy in each caper! Oh, how they flow.
With twists and turns that shine so bright,
Unwritten lines spark the comedy light.

The Silent Narrator's Voice

Whispers echo from the cover's seam,
The narrator giggles, or so it seems.
With every hiccup, a grin is bound,
In silent raucous where joy is found.

Plot holes widen like a comic's face,
As wacky pigeons invade our space.
The author gasps at their own surprise,
As chaos rumbles and laughter flies.

A spoon of soup turns to a plot device,
Where fish talk back and the bread thinks twice.
With every twist, you must hold on tight,
For laughter's the key to this wild delight.

Let's celebrate chaos, fill up your cup,
As the silent narrator won't give up.
In tales where silliness reigns as the king,
Join us in laughter, let the fun begin!

Inkblots on the Canvas of Time

In a world where the clocks tick fast,
We scribble stories that never last.
Characters dance in a coffee stain,
Whispering secrets of joy and pain.

Plot holes like Swiss cheese appear,
As we laugh and share a cold beer.
With every sip, a twist we find,
Was that even a line or a state of mind?

Our hero trips over a garden gnome,
While searching for a place called home.
Mashed potatoes play hide and seek,
Oh, the absurdity makes us squeak!

When the chapter ends, we just flip the page,
With a wink and a grin, we engage.
Each inkblot a clue, a jest in disguise,
Tangled in laughter, we rise and rise.

The Unspooled Storyline

A spaghetti plot that twists and turns,
With red sauce scenes that sizzle and burn.
Characters pop like balloons full of air,
In a world of chaos, beyond compare.

Every moment's a quirky delight,
Where the cat wears a hat and gives fright.
Narratives unravel, then tangle again,
Like a sock that's lost its nearest friend.

The author chuckles with each crazy twist,
As the protagonist swears they can't be missed.
In a room full of socks, what is the clue?
Maybe it's just time for a coffee brew!

The pages are crumpled, a whimsical mess,
But somehow we love the sheer nonsense.
With every laugh, the storyline bends,
More confounding fun till the very end.

Clues in the Everyday

In the crumbs of a cookie, a riddle lies,
With every nibble, a new surprise.
Spilled milk forms tales on the kitchen floor,
As we hunt for clues while we grin and explore.

The toaster's a sage with its popping sound,
Telling tales of lost toast that can't be found.
A sock in the fridge, what's going on?
Our everyday moments are never gone!

Each glance around is an open book,
With secrets hiding in every nook.
Unraveled yarn tells stories untold,
We giggle at mischief that's bright and bold.

The trash can whispers its great debate,
While the cat plots its takeover fate.
Clues in the mundane, they come alive,
In the grand saga where silliness thrives.

Endless Plot Twists

Just when you think you've got it all figured,
A llama walks in, its fate's been triggered.
It juggles bananas and winks with glee,
As characters trip and tumble with glee.

The detective snoozes, the villain trips,
Spilling their plans and sailing on ships.
An octopus hides in a teacup wide,
Confounding the logic we thought we'd bide.

In a storybook world where cows play cards,
And the fish wear shoes made of sweet yard.
Twists keep on spinning, no end in sight,
As laughter erupts at the wild delight.

Chapters unfold with a wink and a twist,
Each absurd detail begs to be missed.
In this boundless tale, we find the cheer,
Where fun shines brightly throughout the year.

Forks in the Road of Fate

A fork in the road, oh what a sight,
Should I go left or take a right?
With each step forward, I wear a grin,
Guess I'll just choose and hope to win!

A squirrel runs by, with nuts in tow,
Seems he's more certain, but where'd he go?
I trip on a root, laugh at my grace,
It's just a detour to a funny place!

Maps are for folks who can read the signs,
But I bring a pizza, that's my only line!
Bumping into clues, and silly folks too,
Every twist and turn leads to laughter anew!

"Oh fate, you quirky little sprite,
You twist and you turn, day and night!
But with every giggle, every mistake,
I find that my journey's the best piece of cake!

Characters Yet to Be Created

In the story I write with a splash of ink,
There's a cat in a hat, oh what do you think?
He juggles fish while riding a bike,
And dances with penguins; it's quite the hike!

Characters emerge from the wildest dreams,
Like a toaster who sings, or a frog that gleams.
They bicker and banter, but who's keeping score?
With capes made of bubble wrap, always wanting more!

With every new plot twist, new friends appear,
A chicken in heels who draws quite a cheer.
Together we chuckle as we weave this thread,
In worlds never mapped, where all fear to tread!

So bring on the laughter, let's turn the page,
Where characters revel in their quirky stage.
Let's scribble and giggle till the ink runs dry,
For every good yarn must somehow apply!

Unfinished Tales of the Soul

In a book on the shelf, with pages untold,
Lurk stories of heroes, both daring and bold.
There's one with a donut who dreams to fly,
And another with socks who just can't say why!

Each tale is a puzzle, with pieces astray,
Like searching for shoes on a muddy up day.
There's laughter in chaos, confetti in pain,
Turning frowns into giggles like sunshine after rain!

From cat-gurus preaching the art of the nap,
To robots who fumble and plot every trap.
The chapters may linger, but life's a good jest,
And every mishap's a reason to rest!

So grab your red pen, let's mark the draft,
For unfinished tales often yield the best craft.
With characters daft and stories so droll,
We'll dance in the margins, it's good for the soul!

The Puzzle of Tomorrow's Dawn

Tomorrow's dawn, a jigsaw to solve,
Like mixing up socks in a wardrobe evolve.
The pieces all scatter, as birds take their flight,
I chase them with coffee, it'll be all right!

With a cat on my lap and crumbs on my jeans,
I try to fit shapes that don't fit in the scenes.
"Is this corner a heart or a slice of pie?"
My puzzle's a circus, and I'm the wrong guy!

The sun peeks in, with its golden light,
Illuminating chaos and pure delight.
So I'll build with the bits that seem out of place,
And stitch a wild tapestry to fill up the space!

As pieces start blending and laughter ignites,
I'll toast to the mayhem and curious sights.
For within every puzzle, a riddle makes fun,
In the madness of dawn, we laugh 'til we run!

Reflections on a Blank Page

A blank page waits with bated breath,
Hoping for a plot or a witty theft.
Characters dance in the author's mind,
Each twist and turn, a riddle designed.

Ink spills like coffee on a Monday morn,
Suddenly, a wild idea is born.
But wait! That character just slipped away,
Leaving the writer in disarray.

Trapped in a plot with no clear end,
Chasing ideas like an old, lost friend.
The pen is a sword, the paper a shield,
Yet stories escape before they are sealed.

So here's to the scribbles, the nonsense plots,
A tale of laughter, and tangled knots.
Turn the page, and just let it flow,
For who needs an ending? Just watch it grow!

The Infinite Unfolding

In a story where no one knows the score,
Characters trip, and the plot hits the floor.
The cat in the hat, the frog in a shoe,
Wondering where all the good chapters flew.

The twists are tangled like spaghetti on a plate,
Do we follow the clues or simply wait?
Each page a puzzle, a witty charade,
With words that jump like they're in a parade.

A page here, a page there, not much to sort,
Mistaken identities in a comical court.
The villain forgets why he's tied up the hero,
Laughs at the chaos, can't help but be a zero.

So we turn the pages with laughter and cheer,
Counting the mishaps, the joy, and the fear.
For in this grand tale, we wander and play,
An infinite unfolding in a silly way!

Prologues of Tomorrow's Secrets

Tomorrow's secrets, tucked in a verse,
Promises and jokes make the plot disperse.
Characters dart like fireflies in night,
Chasing their tails, they take off in flight.

With each prologue, a hint of delight,
The twist of fate or the pulse of fright.
But does the author even know what's next?
Or just tosses words like puzzles perplexed?

In coffee-stained pages, tales intertwine,
With riddles and jokes that bend, realign.
Each laugh a clue, a twist of the quill,
Chasing the meaning like a cat on a hill.

So we scribble and giggle, plot points collide,
With comical turns as the characters ride.
Tomorrow's secrets are where we find glee,
Prologues of laughter, just wait and see!

The Unwritten Dialogues of Today

Today is a book with pages so bare,
Whispers of topics floating in air.
Characters muse, 'What should we say?'
While words play tag and get lost on the way.

Conversations that bubble like soda in cups,
Chasing each other, just never gives up.
The puns and the quips, they wander around,
In the space between silence, they frolic and bound.

Each unwritten dialogue hangs in suspense,
With an awkward pause and a touch of pretense.
Characters grinning, unsure of the scene,
Plotting their antics like playful sardines.

So let's cheers to the gabs we compose,
To stories unwritten where chaos just grows.
For in every jest and each word that's at play,
Lies the magic of today, come what may!

Clues Hidden in Everyday Moments

In the fridge, a pickle's sly grin,
Hiding secrets of what lies within.
A sock escapes, it's on the run,
As the cat plots its next bit of fun.

The postman grins with a newspaper stack,
While my pencil vanishes, it won't come back.
The toast pops up, a breakfast surprise,
With a jammed lid, it's time to improvise.

A shadow's lurking behind the chair,
I suspect the ghost of my last repair.
A coffee spill, the evidence clear,
An artist's touch, or am I just queer?

A dropped call, my phone's got a game,
Texting me riddles that sound quite the same.
Everyday antics, both big and small,
In this wacky novella, we're having a ball!

A Story Without a Finale

The clock won't tick, it just winks at me,
As chapters unfold with bizarre glee.
My cereal dances, but what's its plot?
A twist in every bite, or just a lot?

My shoelaces tangle, a plot thickens fast,
Each step I take feels like a blast.
In the garden, weeds form their own crew,
Plotting to overthrow my tulips anew.

The neighbor's dog claims he's a detective,
Sniffing out stories, always selective.
In the silence of night, I hear my phone,
With ghosts of texts I've never known.

An empty cup, where's the coffee gone?
A missing mystery, just like a con.
With no grand ending, just joyful fumbles,
This tale goes on, as each heart humbles.

Unsolved Riddles of the Heart

A wink from a stranger, was it a clue?
Or just misplaced vision, a heart on the brew?
Confused expressions in a crowded hall,
Are we all just jesters having a ball?

A love note written in ketchup stains,
On a napkin, oh what silly gains!
The pizza guy chuckles, a side quest revealed,
As romantic dinners get all concealed.

Packed in the pantry, an old jar of jam,
Each spoonful whispers, "Who gives a damn?"
Dancing with shadows, twirling with dreams,
The heart's own riddles burst at the seams.

In the park, where the ducks form a band,
I try to decipher their secret plan.
With every quack, there's a longing to cheer,
Unsolved riddles of the heart draw near!

Interludes in the Vast Unknown

A sock emerges from the depths of a drawer,
Is it a traveler from days of yore?
Mismatched, it laughs at its newfound fame,
While my favorite pen plays a disappearing game.

On the TV screen, a plot twist appears,
Invoicing my patience, throughout the years.
The cat's got an agenda, just look at that stance,
In this interlude, there's no second chance.

The fridge hums a tune, could it be a band?
Performing for leftovers they can't quite stand.
Each meal's a story of triumph and loss,
In the vast unknown, we all take a toss.

As my laundry spins, it's a ride or die,
With socks chasing tales, oh my, oh my!
In this endless romp, oh what a thrill,
Interludes unfold, and we love them still!

Prologue and Epilogue Intertwined

In the beginning, we toss a coin,
Each flip a laugh, our fates join.
A plot twist here, a plot twist there,
Who knew life's script would lead to a bear?

Chapters unfold with snacks in hand,
Each bumbling hero makes a stand.
With every turn, you trip and slide,
Wondering how you took that ride!

Comic relief in the strangest place,
A jester dances without grace.
The author chuckles, pen in tow,
Waiting for the next one to throw!

So we turn the page and pause a while,
Every ending sparks a guffaw and smile.
With coffee stains and dreams to blend,
We start again where we may just bend.

Serendipity's Hidden Writings

The ink smudged, a silly sprawl,
Adventures beckon, come one, come all.
Accidental joy in every scribble,
A misfit story, wild and ribble.

A crossword clue leads to a dance,
A hamster running in a chance.
We stumble upon a treasure true,
To find it's just a left shoe or two!

Forgotten voices near the rack,
Each one whispers, 'Don't turn back!'
An open window, a sudden gust,
The plot thickens with playful thrust.

In sketches rough and pages torn,
We find our way in laughter worn.
So write a new line, let chaos reign,
In this humorous riddle, lose that mundane!

The Horizon of Unknown Realms

On the edge of dawn, a cat takes flight,
Chasing sunbeams, quite the sight!
With coffee spilled and dreams up high,
The horizon smiles, it's worth a try.

Every day's a quest, laced with cheer,
Each stumble echoes a joyful sneer.
Maps of mayhem, laughter our key,
Unlocking doors to where we're free!

The seagulls squawk, their drama grand,
Plotting adventures beside the sand.
We're all just actors, backstage blown,
In a cosmos where whimsy has grown.

So take a breath, let silly reign,
In realms unknown, we'll dance in the rain.
With laughter loud and hearts that soar,
Every twist reveals a bit more lore!

Traces of Forgotten Stories

Dusty shelves hold tales of yore,
The stories linger, out to explore.
A dragon sneezes, sending up smoke,
The knight just giggles, he's quite the bloke!

Lost socks whisper from deep in the drawer,
Each one recalls adventures galore.
A tangle of threads, they weave and spin,
A narrative where the wild folks win!

Signs with riddles hang on the wall,
Mistaking a cat for the fairy's ball.
The clock ticks twice, then giggles in glee,
As time plays tricks, no one's quite free.

So gather 'round with a grin so wide,
For in every blink, new pages reside.
With every chuckle and mystery found,
Life's colorful tapestry knows no bound.

Climbing Walls of Uncertainty

I'm scaling walls of things unknown,
Hoping for answers, yet all alone.
Turn another page, but what's the score?
Plot twist awaits, who knows what's in store?

Characters wander, bump into me,
With wacky hats and a sense of glee.
Chasing clues in the cat's lost paw,
Laughing at mysteries, it's all quite raw.

I try to decipher this endless jest,
Jokes that make sense, but never the best.
A fortune cookie's wisdom, what could it be?
"Ask the goldfish," it said with glee.

So I consult the fish, its bowl in a spin,
"Ask not what you seek, but what's hidden within."
As if wisdom lurks in bubbles and fizz,
Just my luck, the fish forgot what it is.

I find my way through riddles and rhymes,
Solving puzzles that mess with my times.
What's next on the list? A dance with a broom?
In the tale of the absurd, I'm facing my doom!

The Unfolding Plot of Now

In the thick of chaos, I take a seat,
With popcorn at hand, the plot's bittersweet.
Characters wander without much a clue,
I'm laughing at scripts they think are so new.

A twist in the tale, they trip on the plot,
Each mistake they make, oh, a comedic shot!
The hero's grand speech, but it's full of fluff,
In scenes of confusion, it's never enough.

Just when I think I've got it all mapped,
A squirrel in a cape, and I'm utterly zapped.
With each page I turn, I giggle with glee,
What's next in this farce? A talking small tree?

Flipping the chapters, all wacky and wild,
Dressed in polka dots like a confused child.
Heroes and villains, what a mixed-up lot,
In this fun little saga, confusion's the plot.

Dusk Without a Closure

The sun sinks low; where does it go?
Chasing shadows in a colorful flow.
The ending is missing, it's such a tease,
Dusk cracks jokes with the evening breeze.

Stars blink down like they've had a drink,
Whispering secrets that make me think.
No finale in sight, just laughs in the air,
I'd ask for a hint, but there's no one to share.

Night tells its tales of wonderful cheer,
A raccoon in shades, what's it doing here?
With a wink and a grin, it twirls in delight,
We dance with the moon in the absence of light.

Each moment absurd, with a dose of surprise,
Chasing twilight, we giggle and rise.
What's next on this trip? I'd love another round,
In a plot without endings, the laughter is found!

The Arcane Scripts of Time

Time scribbles notes on the back of my hand,
In messy handwriting, a faraway land.
Each tick of the clock is a comedic jest,
As days run amok, I'm clearly a guest.

Puzzles wrapped up with no present to unpack,
I laugh at the chaos; who's keeping track?
A wardrobe full of clothes, all mismatched styles,
Dressing up tomorrow in today's goofy smiles.

The script keeps changing, the actors don't learn,
Each scene feels like spaghetti, twisted and turned.
With each act's arrival, I take out my pen,
To rewrite the tale, just for the fun of it then.

Inscribed in the margins, in ink that is bold,
"Don't take it too seriously; it's all been foretold."
The beauty of nonsense is simply divine,
In the arcane scripts, I'm enjoying the line.

www.ingramcontent.com/pod-product-compliance
Lightning Source LLC
Chambersburg PA
CBHW051637160426
43209CB00004B/686